ROLL CALL

DAYS OF WAR ANTHOLOGY

Roll Call; Days of War Anthology

Editor and Compiler: Ronda Wicks Eller (1965 -)
Cover and Interior Artist: Ronda Wicks Eller (1965 -)

Foreword
Poems Index
Author Bios

I.S.B.N. 978-1-9990964-5-8
First Edition 2019

Published by SkyWing Press, Clinton, Ontario, Canada.

SkyWing Press
Poetry in Flight
skywingpress@gmail.com

Foreword

How does one begin to write about a book on this theme? It would be great to say that we, the whole world over, have learned our lesson about how war kills physically, emotionally and in spirit too. If it resolves anything, it can liberate the oppressed or defend the innocent but far too often we see that it has been used as a political manoeuvre with corporate advantage (where, under the guise of liberation, acquisitions are the real goal).

The object of this book is to remember the men, women and families that lost lives and/or loved ones in wars of liberation but I would be remiss if we were not to include the people who have incurred the same losses, having been victims of war enacted for regime conquest or as unwitting pawns in other great schemes. As a new millennium, global society that prides itself on progressive thought and advancement it is a wonder that war continues to exist at all, yet it does. Humans are still assaulting one another and that is sad, but that isn't the point of this book - it is only something to remember and reflect on while reading it.

The poems in this anthology are interesting and thought-provoking, full of variety in style, thoughtfulness and mood from contributors who have contemplated war, remembered family members lost and put themselves in the proverbial shoes of others who lived it firsthand, and some are veterans. As we approach Remembrance Day 2019 there is great insight and gratitude for the liberties we enjoy, to be gleaned through remembering people past and present that made, and are making, sacrifices on our behalf. Until the entire world lives without war and oppression...

We Must Remember Them.

I would like to personally thank Donna Allard of New Brunswick, Canada, International Beat Poet Laureate for the National Beat Poetry Foundation Inc., Connecticut, U.S.A., for her time reading and adjudicating this collection without knowing which poems were submitted by their respective contributors. Roll Call; Days of War is SkyWing Press' first anthology competition and I am very pleased with this result.

Ronda Wicks Eller.
SkyWing Press

Index

Military Balance

He was born;

in Toronto	in Kabul
democratic childhood	war zone youth
nurtured sunrise	feared sunrise sky
excelled in school	scavenged to exist
developed life skills	survived in hellish want
teenage enjoyment	hungered for comfort
a young man	learned explosive techniques
in the pursuit of love	adrenaline hatred
learned many a sport	taught to operate weapons
loved a challenge	target practice
became a pilot	how to target a plane
joined the Air Force	entered a militia
assigned a fighter jet	drove a jeep
guns, bombs, and missiles	of light air-bound missiles
upon a mission zone	from the sky
zeroed in on the enemy	came an enemy
devastated the target zone	shells and tracer fire
vehicles and people blasted	sudden great pain
pulled up for departure altitude	his body blown skyward
back to the base	landed dead hard
soft landing to recuperation	now to a makeshift funeral
he is the child of a mom	he was the child of a mom

~ Ed Woods

Sonnet No. 5
Why

New morning sun brings forth her warming rays
while dying leaves drift gently to the ground.
Approaching winter soon will dampen days,
when ice will hang from barren trees abound.
Korea's changing beauty I have seen,
penned every scene for all the world to read.
I miss so much your sparkling eyes of green,
while for your love, my heart again will bleed.
The freezing snow will cover all that lives
I hope I will survive this daily fight.
A priest once said that Jesus Christ forgives,
though what I do, he could not see as right.
My helmet sits upon my weary head -
My rifle, now replaces pencil lead.

~ David J. Delaney

For my Uncle, Lawrence George Delaney, 1st Battalion RAR,
who served in Korea.

New Generation Veterans

We honour our old veterans, we honour them with pride
and read of all the horrors they have carried deep inside.
We know they served in Asia or New Guinea's highland rains,
Vietnam or in Africa where, many men were slain.

We know that fateful landing on Gallipoli's dark shore,
wherever Aussies fought, we know there are so many more,
but now a new young generation needs our help as well,
they too have been to war and suffer with their private hell.

Though losses aren't classed as great, their fears are the same
those electronic hidden bombs, still injure, kill or maim.
They fight against an enemy they find so hard to see
who mingle in the market place, then cause much tragedy.

Insurgents in Afghanistan hide in the rough terrain
or roaming in Iraq, where, wearing robes they look the same.
These suicide stealth bombers, don't care who they hurt or kill,
then, with their own beliefs, they try to break our forces will.

Our fighting Aussie spirit shows on any foreign land,
they're in the skies, they're on the sea, or on the desert sand.
Now many are returning with the horrors they still see
and living with their nightmares, suffering bureaucracy.

I know on ANZAC day, we all remember with a tear,
but all vets young or old, they need our help throughout the year,
support and listen to their stories, when they do get told,
lets honour our new veterans, just like we do our old.

~ David J. Delaney

Our Shapes Eternal
(on hearing about poets fighting in the Syrian Civil War)

This tension is not a tension
I have ever known.

It is a ligature pulled white
a noose chasing light
pressing the kite tight
against the muscled clouds
a filament fixed
like a sharp bright bit
held fast in these spittled mouths
we use to proclaim our cause
through the confused milk
of our poetry.

But the revolution went well today.

We're winning back the farms
and while the cities are our hearts
the farms are the sinews of our hands
braided by generations
into the stubborn twine of our resistance.

And now we rest in this shaded grove
where the olives fall like wizened planets at our feet.

The heat in its clinging weave
marinates the shadows into oily ghosts.
The bees among the stalls of twilight
drone their lazy hymns where the citrus drifts.

Know this my brothers

we are not soldiers or fighters with ready blades
not warriors with the tools of our killing
worn as bloodied flags on raging sleeves.

We are lovers
at best poets

the poets of some lost and broken line
the guardians of a dying rhyme

who in our misery
raise high the flaccid scythes of our words
so empty our art
so empty our love
against this war
and the inky swirl of our dreaming.

A trumpet sounds the chorus call
to join the battle once again.

And as one we poets rise
like a quiet healing tide
singular in our prayer
that this night our words
will have the strength they'll need
to carry us toward another dawn.

Our march toward the town is long.

We leave among the olive trees
only the blackened stubs of our cigarettes

the bees among the daisies droning

and our shapes
like fossils deep in amber
pressed eternally on the waving grass.

~ David Stones

Previously published in Synaeresis 5, Harmonia Press, 2018

A Brief History of Expatriation
~For Thomas and George Youden, Lost at Sea, January, 1915

Thomas Youden sailed from England
in 1820, landed in Brigus in a harsh new land.
A master mariner and watchmaker by trade,
he was appointed principal of Newfoundland's
first consolidated school, spent his evenings
teaching navigation to the next generation of sailors.
He built a home in Bull Cove and raised a family
that would flourish for generations. He spoke
with an English accent, was born in a foreign land
but no one called him an immigrant, they called him
a pioneer.

In 1914 the world was at war, two of Bull Cove's
finest answered the call for mother England, set sail
on the armed merchant vessel HMS Viknor.
They struck a German mine and went down off the coast
of Ireland, their bodies were never found.
They're recognized as the first North American casualties
of the Great War, the British government erected
a monument to honor their courage, everyone bowed
their heads in remembrance of those brave men
from faraway lands. They spoke with peculiar accents
but from the streets of London to the far corners
of the English countryside no one called them foreigners,
they called them heroes.

I was born in a sovereign land, a man of two provinces,
I speak with the strangest of accents, a broken English infused
with Acadian slang. My ancestors arrived from distant lands
but no one calls me a foreigner, my father was born
in a British colony but no one calls him an immigrant.
On July 1st when the flag is raised two hundred years
of history screams through my veins, it's the story of a nation
built on the blood, sweat and tears of trailblazers and pioneers
who fought to keep the dream alive.
For Thomas and George, my heart beats Canadian
and it's bursting with pride, these words are my blood
splattered to page, red as our nations flag.

~ Philip Youden

Red Cross Cutting Rooms

Upstairs, we trace patterns
on the top surface, slice through
wads of cloth 175 folds thick
more easily than through butter,

the round blade's electric hum
a prelude for warm garments
sewn to console soldiers overseas
who have not yet suffered.

Downstairs, we cut bandages
and wind them into rolls,
bandages for wounds deep
as those in hearts back home.

~ Meg Freer

Previously published in Arborealis: A Canadian Poetry Anthology,
compiled by John B. Lee, Beret Days Press, The Ontario Poetry
Society, 2019

Bounty

chalk white fingers
reach up through muck
yellow lard peeled away from bone
congealing in a pond
warm as life
black as death

steel saucers
till bone and sinew
into fields of dirt -
wounds healed over
forgotten

cold earth pitted
by cannon fire and shrapnel
soon covered by thatch of green
thin bristles give way to stalks
their heads heavy
bent from a generation's blood
a nations solemn tears

a crop so rich
filling plates to brim
mouths to scream
with joy at good fortune
not seen since
before the Somme

~ Trish Shields

This poem is about the human remains that are being unearthed in old battlefields around the world. In this case they were found in the rich soil of farmlands and developing properties in France.

Buried Deep

(details from a memoir by Sergeant Jim Alexander, MM,
Lincoln and Welland Regiment, Holland, 1945.)

In the kitchen, from the doorway to the hearth,
lying on the floor like some colossal cigarette—
a log, one end in the fire, burning slowly
as flames surround a bubbling pot.

It mystified the Canadian soldiers, those kept
after the war—troops retained
to rebuild a battered country, one that refused
to be swallowed back into the sea.

The explanation provided to the curious,
Because the Nazis took all of our metal:
axes, pitchforks, scythes and hoes, even kitchen knives—
a last ditch effort to build more weapons.

Allied saviours shared meals of boiled tulip bulbs:
'the most gawd-awful things you ever ate'
along with Red Cross chocolate and rationed tins
of bully beef: bitter meals of freedom.

Under our barn, wrapped in oiled burlap,
we have our tractor and plow—buried bits cloistered away
following the final swoop of the flag of black on red.
They never found them. Soon, we will plant.

~ Becky Alexander

*Previously published in the Cambridge Wartime Scrapbook, ON,
2005, translated into Dutch for a newspaper in Netherlands, in
Shrapnel, Tales of a Soldier Dad by Becky Alexander, Craigleigh
Press, Ontario, 2009 and Tamaracks, Canadian Poetry for the 21st
Century, Lummox Press, California, 2018.*

Night Taxi

Christmas Eve night shift
"taxi-taxi" I heard
across the street a lone man
pointed to stop near

he got in the front seat
no gift bags or boxes
nor in the Christmas spirit

directions accepted
I wished him Merry Christmas
he cried in wail and thanked me
and said he recognized me
but I differed

he referred to years before
in a POW camp
soldiers at a barrack door
he cowered in corner stale stench
it's their time for entertainment
his time for amusement execution

one soldier disarmed himself
"Canadians" they stated
"the war is over for you"
comforted and coaxed outside
to see others in tearful dance
his near collapse relief in disbelief

time to return home free
his town was bombed flat
Canada was his choice
to start a new life

tonight in kind words
brought back memories
of other Canadian boys

~ Ed Woods

High Ground (WWI and WWII)

We met the birds long before Hitchcock
even though the flap of their wings
was buried in that of flags
and pounding hearts,
and the constant drone of Lee Enfields
echoing through the front lines -
shaping bloody pools as bird baths.

We heard our voices calling out
for the gentle breasts of women,
any woman who could draw us
back beyond our trench nest,
back into the womb where
we might plead with God
for yet another round.

It didn't happen.

Instead, we watched our buddies
being carried up to the high ground,
lain in bushels like cobs of corn
and placed on trucks heading over
to a some market owned by Flanders
who traded in wooden boxes
and poppy seeds

to which the birds
finally came.

~ Ronda Wicks Eller

*The Lee Enfield is a bolt-action, magazine-fed, repeating rifle
that was the main firearm used by the military forces of the British
Empire and Commonwealth from 1895 until 1957.
** The Birds is a 1963 American horror film by Alfred Hitchcock.*

Gods of War
(In Memory of Brendan Scott Leise)

Kartikeya. Horus. Ares. I summon you all.
Agurzil. Bishamon. Mars.
I gnash my teeth at the fall of a heart
that still beats with a pulse in my mind.
Of a face in this world that I will never again find.

His blood is on your hands. His blood is on your hands.

Mesopotamia? What unfinished business had he there?
His mind had been plagued by the poisoned air.
Many men had ventured to her and returned in despair.
The Furies had left no refuge
for a friend who saved me from our own walking war.
He waits on the other side of an impenetrable door
that I stand at the entrance to.
I pound and I beat until my fists become sore
and there is never an answer, and we
always need someone to blame for Seppuku.
We blamed it on your mother, we blamed it
on your father,we blamed it on the valkyrie
that left your gun wounded body on the battlefield.

His blood is on your hands. His blood is on your hands.

How often I slumber, thinking of all the ways I could
have picked up your pieces from the ground,
as if you were manna that hailed from the sky
and let the birds consume you from my open palms.
They'd deliver your remains to the feet
of the gods of war, where you would be honored.

I stand at the mouth of the Mnemosyne
making myself sick from crimson waters
trying to find a way to bring you back.
My lips long for the cool drip of the Lethe river, but
there is no solace in forgetting everything.

From opposite sides of one door we both scream,
doomed to only be together during the fickleness of
dream.

~ *Vanessa Rowan Whitfield*

the dystopia of eagles
(drone in my own tears)

once fiercely beautiful
proud and independent
the eagle loses face

an invasive species
the hawks of America
spread terror worldwide

even great nations tremble
anticipate worse to come
hawks spread their wings

the hawks of America
smell the fear and blood
hunt ever further afield

hawks spread their wings
bald eagles come to roost
lose respect and grace

boys hide deep in a bunker
send virtual hawks flying
destroying other worlds

~Bob MacKenzie

Kursk - July, 1943

the roiling, up-heaved earth, disturbed
gives up its pulped men on fire
shouts turning into muffled groans
in its earthen breast of rain-drenched mire

thirteen thousand rumbling tanks
twelve thousand aircraft, bullets flew
four million men, warrior women, too
hurled against steely, flaming jaws
of lumbering, mechanical brutes
unleashed with shredding blasts
exacting pains, treads mangling flesh
muting moans, imprinted tracks
on soaking ground with blood remains.

from east defence to west advance
the Tigers burning; hulks remaining
from each other at gun barrel range
Operation Citadel was thus interred
T-34s moved westward undeterred
rattling, hammering, clanging
their turrets thirsting blood
to extirpate, eviscerate and liberate.

back home our collective soul engages
in fear, loss, suffering and heroics
our sense of justice salutes and kneels
to all those fields of battles from our past
endless keening through the years
plucking at our memory scars
heeding now the peace dove's peals
but, once more, Guernica's war horse
teeth bared, rears and reels
as we stanch past bleeding
as we keep weeding as flowers bloom
from seeding our families' graves.

~ Lisa Makarchuk

*The largest tank battle in human history, one major turning point
of WWII, was at Kursk, July, 1943. This poem is to honour all who
fought there, including thirteen relatives who died in this war.*

Holocaust Cemetery
~ On visiting the Zaglembier Monument

Grass and mud mingle
in trodden sorrow
around the granite.

Beloved names
of the dead
etched in Yiddish,
like a story by Sholem Aleichem
written in Auschwitz.

Engraved columns
bitterly sleep
on a slate grey landscape
in the orphaned park
without a voice
or a dream.

The sun is buried too
under swollen clouds
the compressing sky
near tears
and the wind clings
to my legs
like a frightened child.

The air is in pain
its dull white grasping breath
makes the minutes crawl
in naked trembling silence.

~ I. B. Iskov

Search and Destroy

I follow a column of tanks
hidden as a rattlesnake
my tank turret and shells
about to strike danger

numbered units
unaware of their count
full of battle weary souls
about to ascend or descend
to their final rest

the first one turns off
a fatal move
it quickly explodes
next I light up
the last one
others will be lit up
in congested order

in celebration
my mobile circumference
moves on for the next
search and destroy

~ Ed Woods

On Page Eleven

Like a school girl, with a crush,
she wrote his name on page eleven
of her puzzle book, hidden in the sudoku,
tucked into the basket of her walker.
She wondered, would her soldier boy remember
the letter she sent him seventy years ago?

He wondered when he got that letter.
There were no cross words
only goodbye and his picture.
He's forgotten her name
but the puzzle remains:
did she ever love him?

~ Wendy MacLean

The Brig

I may come and go as I please
if I wave my hand nicely.
Tuesdays and Fridays we get fish,
eyes baked in the heads.

Lifers say you can't have a jail
unless there is something
worth caging.
This is how I know I matter.

Sundays we have a social
if it isn't raining.
I wear a rat catcher blazer.

A few friends come over.
Bruce shows me his jail--
lines hypothesized on clay
in the shape of a cage.

Visiting my plain-spoken hutch,
he wonders what I could have done
to earn a second pillow.

On clear days we can see
a distant road, houses, a store,
smoke plumes, a cemetery where
all the lieutenants are buried.

~ Barrett Warner

previously published in Consequence Magazine, 2015

War Dance

September strolls
through centennial park
along a muddy path
where I witness the battle zone:
each tree a brilliant flag of colors
each tree a country of its own
its leaves falling one by one
into foreign territory
once waving from lofty boughs
they blend into landscape,
wilting, becoming fossils

reaching into a lottery of leaves,
I pick a winner, and
cut into its surface with the word
"war"
the ruddy sap on red barely legible
bleeding leafy-veins that make me think
of you, and my parents too

there's a brisk feel to the air today--
the leaves are flitting, dancing about,
soon snowflakes will blanket them
then summer will bring blossoms
and bird song. once again I will
travel to my hometown cemetery

to view the granite thumb marks
that identify you among the dead.
funny how we quarter the years
25 - 50 - 75 - 100 and how
we quarter the seasons too,

how I always dread leaving you
alone in death, but sometimes
i feel nothing and then I dance
like a leaf, I dance-dance-dance.

~ Donna Allard

Previously published in Cold Fire
- Donna Allard, SkyWing Press, Ontario, 2019

February 18, 1968

I saw no rocket's red glare,
hearing only the whistling hiss
a millisecond before the thunderclap
knocked me to the floor,
filled my eyes with death's dust,
dammed my ears with silence

Anyone hit?

I felt no pain, yet blood
spattered across my shirt,
leaving me to wonder
if shock dulled my senses;
Only when I wiped away
the gritty particles
did I realize pieces of hot metal
had slashed his organs
and innards from their moorings,
spilling them into a bloody pool

That night we congregated
at my bunk, dissecting our loss
as a doctor might autopsy a cadaver;
"He didn't know what hit him"
"He didn't suffer"
"He didn't cry out for his mother"
No mutation of the language
made Rick any less dead, did it?

I was among many drinking
himself to sleep that night,
yet hoping sedation by alcohol
would not render us helpless
if acts of random violence
interrupted our rendezvous
with Hypnos and Somnos
who too often begrudgingly
offered their treasured gift

by next morning the space
had been cleansed of blood,
two workmen squatted

on their haunches,
affixing pristine panels
onto the floor; one of the men
put a nail through the untucked
tail of the other's shirt
and when the aggrieved man stood,
the shirt responded
with a clean tear reaching
to the garment's collar;
He cursed at the top of his lungs
in that language we knew
a smattering of words;
The other returned the curses
and we all laughed, wondering
if this act reminiscent
of an ancient vaudeville sketch
was meant to induce our amusement
and lighten the tension
we felt than and beyond

~ Mark Fleisher

Previously published in "Reflections:Soundings from the Deep (2018), Mercury Heartlink, Albuquerque and Silver City, NM, USA

A War Haiku

Fragments of metal
invading his innocence
He comes home too soon

~ Mark Fleisher

Previously published in Moments of Time (2014), Mercury Heartlink, Albuquerque and Silver City, NM, USA

Sunshine of Beer

There is sunshine in the taste of beer:
of a June wheat day, blonde grain kissing
the cerulean blue sky, and a 103 temperature
baking the green enamel
of a John Deere 55 H combine.

It is the smell of bread brewing on the prairie wind.

The farmer, cabless with his Coors,
babysitting his girls in the bin of the combine,
perched above the churning gears.

There were so many ways to die that day:
in the jaws of the combine, sliding
on cracked vinyl seats without a seatbelt,
riding the tipping truck, dumping wheat
at the grain elevator, hoping the elevator man
would give us a stick of gum.

OSHA never knew and KCSL never cared
about us sipping the last swallow of daddy's beer.
They never knew it was the farmer who died.

Was it the pink mercury treated wheat in the old JD seed drill?
The Barban (carbyne) for the wild oats?
Or was it the visit to Sasebo, Japan, swabbing the deck of
radiation?

Death blooms from the seeds
Drilled into the ground so long ago.
We are harvested by the deed done wrong,
the accidents unknown, the ignorance of greed.
We become the brewed amber ale drunk down.

~ Barbara A. Meier

Previously published in 2018, "Pure Slush", the Greed issue

Native (Aboriginal) Warrior Pride

alone on this ridge
blue skies suspend clouds
across our heritage

our failing chief prayed to higher spirits
to accept me as his choice
as new tribal leader

invaders never conquered
our beliefs or this place
or howls of a solitary wolf
ice sheets reflected night stars
dusty herds roam
bears in plentiful rapids
teach their young
springtime fishing rights

I recall a time when this land
was full of bountiful life
until the sole predator
of man and bear
arrived on iron rails of change
with the long rifle to seek riches
and trophies from the buffalo hunt

my pride is to uphold
our heritage in trust
with powerful warrior's heart
in mind of conscience
stronger than tomahawk or knife

in time Great Spirits will accept
my soul in a fiery tribute
ashes up to the night sky
as the next warrior chief
stands proud on sacred land

his heart will beat proudly
honored to lead our people
and will stand in admiration
alone on this ridge

~ Ed Woods

Woman With a Cocoa Jug

Relief troops grope through midnight mist
behind the front, when an apparition asks,
"Would you like a drink of cocoa?"
Jug in one hand, milk tin in the other,
a lone woman keeps nightly vigil,
dispenses memories of happy times
from a small alcohol stove
in the broken village of Compiègne.

~ Meg Freer

*After Mrs. George B. Penrose, My monograph: war relief work in
old Louisiana (Himebaugh & Browne, New York, 1919).*

My Father's Medals

My father's medals
are now too heavy
for him to wear.

They weigh down his small chest
stoop him over
with their long tales
of death and boredom
corned beef for breakfast
and body parts steaming
on the Burmese front.

My father despises
what happened to him
over there.

He'll tell you that
settled in his chair
by the window
delivering a reflective swirl
to his beloved CC and ginger
as if the glass itself
holds the stories
he feels so compelled to relate.

My father lost a wife to that war.

He lost his youth
and his innocence
close to sixty pounds
and his very perception
of being.

He gained a few things
as well, I guess.

He learned how to smoke cigarettes
and all about fragility.
He discovered what it means
to treasure
and how distance
intensifies love.

He found out
what's worth fighting for
and what isn't
and not just in terms of the war.

That's what he'll tell you.
He'll tell you exactly that...

in his chair by the window
rotating his rye
until those medals
on his narrow chest
begin to tremble

like leaves

about to fall.

~ David Stones

For dad, Sgt. William Deryck Stones, British Armed Forces, Royal Lincolnshire Regiment, Burmese Front...R.I.P

First published in Infinite Sequels, Friesen Press, 2013

Disposable

my body aches all over
an ordeal just to get out of bed
some days my walker is OK
mostly travel is in a wheelchair
it's all I can do

no lift to get me into a bathtub
a shower is not possible
I have help three times per week
that's all I can afford
as is this dank dingy room

I have become a disposable nuisance
with the level of care I need
from injuries sustained during bailout
from a mega-million dollar jet
ripped apart on a military mission

~ Ed Woods

Double Jeopardy

It was one of those story-and-a-half French farmhouses.
The enemy took advantage of its situation
high on a hill, surrounded by a stout stone wall.
A machine gunner set up
in the window above the main door,
prevented Allied advance.
Shelled for days, and still active,
Dad's section was ordered to knock out the nest.
The plan—for Dad, armed with two grenades—
to jump the wall, toss the grenades
through that high window,
dive through the front door.
Hoping that when the explosives blew,
the solid walls of the house
would provide his protection.
As he flew through the doorway,
he had that famous moment in time,
found himself sailing through the air:
there were no floors left inside the house,
the machine gun set up on an improvised stage.
The instant he hit the cellar floor
he bounced right back up,
leapt through a basement window
just as the explosion hit,
—mission accomplished.

~ Becky Alexander

*Previously published in 'Shrapnel, Tales of a Soldier Dad,' by
Becky Alexander, Craigleigh Press, Cambridge ON, 2009.*

Traveller

at his funeral, standing near his grave
a band plays the Internationale slow
and the few who stand there at his graveside
 sing out still familiar words of hope

he would not have wanted some hippocrite
preaching life everlasting over him
so an old communist speaks of past times
and of fallen nearby forgotten comrades

Lenin and Trotsky stand at his graveside
chilling the hearts they had once filled with hope,
Uncle Joe is banned for being rowdy,
and Karl Marx' words provide the eulogy

recalling Joe Hill and legends of Wobblies
some sing Solidarity Forever;
recalling long ago ideals and passions
others wonder what their lost cause had won

grey men stand around a hole in the earth
tossing in handsful of forgotten dreams,
manifestos, and songs, then silence comes
somewhere near the edge an old woman weeps

~ Bob MacKenzie

*previously published in "somewhere still in wind the tree is
bending", Silver Bow Publishing, New Westminster, 2018;
also published in "Rat's Ass Review," U.S.A.,summer 2018 issue.*

Rape of Nanking
- The Other Holocaust, December 13, 1937

enemy troops entered Nanking
seven weeks of killing ensued
unleashing rape, atrocity
murder and rampage
with hatred imbued

evil harvested the city; it came
in goosesteps of soldiery who claim
a superior race mentality
sharing convenient indifference
and studied acceptance
by those exercising no resistance
to this genocidal existence
what is it in war and battle that happens
soldiers' morality subsumed by flame
while we hear much of the same
in the tiresome but hopeful refrain:
NEVER AGAIN!

~ Lisa Makarchuk

sections previously published in "Buried Horror", January, 2018

Fascination

upon theater screen
beautiful and artistic
flickered black and white
the newsreel called it
a mushroom cloud
trailing birth style cord
- down to total destruction

I sit in fascination
- post-flight photos
- aircraft crew assembled
- Enola Gay

in later years
the scene played much better
in Panavision Technicolor
- never failed to entertain

once of the age to understand
my soul ached in sadness
for the unfortunate innocent
- they never knew what hit them

~ Ed Woods

Monte Cassino

I am the Temple of Apollo, I am known by many names
rebuilt and immortalized then destroyed by old regimes
in Fall of '43 war was once more at my gates
three monks stood and witnessed as walls were laid to waste
in time I felt each fragment painstakingly replaced
returning many icons; the rest have been appraised

I am the Temple of Apollo, I am known by many names
the last monk curls within an alcove with his book of faith
his footsteps are soft against the calm of my embrace
they echo through the halls where icons once were placed

the ancient monk lies sleeping; smiles wreath his wizened face
they warm the autumn air, anointing my holy place
his abiding honour fills the cracks within this place
though lost within reflecting, he is worthy of my grace
while conflict seethes around this hill and many lives erased
I am the Temple of Apollo, I am known by many names

~ Trish Shields

Monte Cassino is a Benedictine Temple in Italy and has existed in one form or another since 529 AD. It became a contentious piece of property in 1943 when US Armed Forces laid a withering barrage upon it in an effort to keep German forces from taking it and making it an impenetrable vantage point. Many religious artifacts and manuscripts were to be transported to the Vatican but 15 cases never arrived; they were given to Hermann Göring on his birthday. All but three Benedictine monks survived the battle yet the temple was rebuilt, using pieces of the original temple that had been rebuilt in 1450.

Homecoming

Wind under a thin rain
smoke in sullen threads
pulled from the chimney pots

a soldier on a porch
comes home.

Ribs like brittle slats
against the khaki's nettles
a man reduced to sparrow bones

as the soldier on the porch
comes home.

Fog lifting across the dales
careful percussion on a forgotten door
just the milkman as witness

when the soldier on the porch
comes home.

Teen departs a Yorkshire town
to lose his youth in Burma
and now this man in the rain

knocking
knocking

as the soldier on the porch
comes home.

~ David Stones

We Did Not Die

We did not die, the veteran whispered ...
some of us got to the ticker-tape parade.

We received our medals in person
and lived as heroes ... for a spell.

We did not die but there were times
our heroism did. Public memories dimmed,

surviving only in our minds,
bearing arms against us,

unpinning grenades, dispersed
in grotesque mental snapshots,

serving horrible memories
as bloody cocktails at bedtime
we could not escape!

Oh yes, we finished the war - but limping,
and few understood our postwar cries

until they heard our metal plates
clash like cymbals on casket floors

and realized we never
entirely made it home
even though we did not die.

~ Ronda Wicks Eller

*In memory of my great grandfather Tom Broadhurst, who served
in WWI, Canadian Regiment. He was shell-shocked while
retrieving injured soldiers and lived the rest of his life with PTSD
and an unsteady gait caused by the metal plate in his head.*

Reunion

WWII fighter plane crash
far from pilot bailout landing
twenty three years old
shot down over Holland
in a war that must be won

shaken and injured
limped a stressful distance
safety found in a barn
hopefully far enough
from the German search area
as no POW's was the rule

under a horse blanket
only the farmer would miss
covered in loft's soft straw
collapsed into near coma sleep

whisper awakened
uniforms expected
machine guns ready
instead a beautiful woman
senior to his years
as close as a kiss
with promise of secrecy

recovery strength improved
closeness seems more often
in lofts remoteness
for undetected allied safety

one day urges overpowered
a soft kiss then apology
apology accepted
she kissed back

battles won homeland security
month's later war victory
war has finally ended
service personnel repatriated

twenty years passed

then oceanic travel
carried him safely
back to the scene
of wartime survival

in a familiar front yard
seemingly unchanged
busy radiant beauty
she turned and glanced
about to ask who

he points to the sky
then towards injured area
they race to embrace
in waterfall tears
stronger kisses not awkward
nor under discovery fear

this day they loved
in an open field

~ Ed Woods

Changi Larrikins

They huddle in the bush, like thieves who strike then flee the fight
and know if they are caught, they'd not survive another night.
Just like a well-drilled team, they're confident and so refined,
then join the other prisoners where they've all been confined.

For fuel is gold and buys supplies that's needed by the men
while all the while they risk of being bashed there once again
but rendezvous they do, for Chinese and tribes pay well,
where, only for a moment they'd forget about their hell.

Though painful death or cruelty for inmates was abound
and any misdemeanour, would bring bashings all around,
or working on that rail line where so many Aussie's died,
they kept their sense of humour and their noted Aussie pride.

Word filtered thru the compound that the commandants flash car,
ran dry of fuel when he approached, the freshly laid black tar.
The only give away, around that god-forsaken place;
a certain group of Aussie's — with huge grins upon each face.

~ David J. Delaney

Based on a true story as told by my step father-in-law, Norm Hutley, who spent 3.5 years in Changi prison camp during world war 2.

Civilian War Hospital in the Abstract

"Never in the history of wars has such a thing been done."

We bring the wounded on stretchers,
out of danger to the first zone,
where they lie alone until we have time
to move only those still alive to the second zone—

barracks, hospital, museum or cathedral—
we the medical corps always prepared
to pack up as the battle hub shifts,
follow after, arrive intact,

all expenses paid by the government,
salaries flowing smooth as velvet
through sorrow and loss, an inspiring idea
of efficiency, "gloriously American".

~ Meg Freer

* After Mrs. George B. Penrose, My monograph: war relief work in
old Louisiana, Himebaugh & Browne, New York, 1919.

Previously published in Arborealis: A Canadian Poetry Anthology, compiled by John B. Lee, Beret Days Book, The Ontario Poetry Society, 2019

Unknown to Us

He was unknown to us
until his name appeared in a list
when I searched for my ancestors.
He died at Vimy.
Nobody called him a hero.
Nobody even mentioned him.

His brother, my grandfather, is still unknown.
His story is lost in the muddied memories
of a child who waited for her father
while she read the news
about the little princesses
and their uncle, who left his crown.
She wanted to be her father's princess
but he didn't leave. He just never came home.

On Remembrance Day
as we honour the unknown soldier
I will think of these two men unknown to me.
Vimy claimed one. Divorce claimed the other.
I will call them uncle and grandfather,
and lay them to rest
with the other casualties of war.

~ Wendy MacLean

refugee blues

you have to grant relief

it took a long time before we asked
till we got used to sleeping on the floor.

you can get used to almost anything.

mostly it's quiet
people are just tired and quiet
and you go back home.

or you go and sit with hundreds of others
or you just up and leave.

here it's like that too
you feel it in the air
 you see it in the eyes.

I don't much care
I just want it to end.

today it was sunny at last
the clouds yesterday were black
and then today sun.

who will rise up against evil
who stand up against iniquity?

there was still the wind
and the cold sun shining.

the breeze got too brisk
so I nodded goodbye
made my way to the moors.

brought back a jar of water.

~ Bob MacKenzie

Previously published in "somewhere still in wind the tree is bending", Silver Bow Publishing, New Westminster, 2018

"We are the dead. Short days ago, we lived."

A stone enclosure demarcates
the official border between nations

veil between realms, a fence entwined
with parched grasses and nettles,

blue chicory blooms powdered white
with gravel spit from tires on another hot

Italian afternoon. At the edge I see the steep
cliffs, the twisted torsos of olive trees, juniper

and cypress. Their camouflage shadows
grope an arduous climb reminiscent of soldiers

disembarking from their ships, time a delirious
haze rising from the coast below, as tourists now

swim and sunbathe unaware, Quite leisurely
from the disaster. And I remember Brueghel's Icarus

falling from the sky In Auden's poem, while the world
kept living. One grief contained in one enchanted view.

at the gate I cannot distinguish the here and there
of things. The then and now. The me and them. Not yet,

although in the shaded vestibule, a historic plaque
instructs with concrete details of casualties and dates.

It hits me only when I step out into the christened time
capsule of this Canadian acreage. The dream-like lawn

of maple trees and oak, of patriotism for flag and country,
a garden of mowed grass so green, trimmed, but not

adorning suburban houses, instead white headstones
with epitaphs that read He is not dead. He is just away.

I recognize their names, the names of boys
I might have known at school, kids playing a game

of heroes instead of hockey or baseball & this park
could be a diamond or a rink, a playing ground walled in.

Canada, home away from home, here in the heart
of my native Abruzzo. The common denominator

for those like me, who call two countries home.
these hills and sea my father and D'Annunzio loved.

where people are rugged and mild like the coast, they too
bear the atrocities of war, their families mutilated

by the posturing standoffs of egomaniacal
leaders. Precious lives spilled too young, dormant

for eternity here, away from Halifax, Toronto, Montreal
Vancouver, Winnipeg. Each tiny town where mom and dad,

Sister, brother, lover, friend forever awaited their return.
What a price to pay for peace!

Maybe one day when I die, we will all meet here or
in Canada, where my parents' graves now consecrate

what was once my foreign soil. Together, we will gather
for a big feast in the sunlight, into that effervescent

aliveness of being, that magic world brimming
with love, neutrinos, dark matter and God.

~ Josie DiSciascio-Andrews

In Italy, December 1943, Canadian forces fought one of
their toughest battles of the war in a bid to capture Ortona. The
month-long campaign, first at the Moro River outside Ortona and
then with vicious street fighting in the town itself, cost more than
2,300 Canadian casualties, but eventually won Ortona for the
Allies. - paraphrased from The Canadian Encyclopedia
    The Moro River Canadian War Cemetery is near the Adriatic
Sea at San Donato (about 5 kms south of Ortona) and the
Province of Chieti, Abruzzo, in Italy. There are 1,615 graves in the
cemetery; over 50 are unidentified and 1, 375 are Canadian.
- paraphrased from Veterans Affairs Canada

Allegiances

I fell silent in awe
a veteran's recollection
loss of innocence
hammered by loss of comrades
life was not so kind

aviation equipment destroyed
midair over enemy territory
few survivors unscathed
prisoners of war horror

he kept spirits high
in survival routine hope
to be homeward bound

war won and liberated
he now treasures each day
as a luxury of living

I see the effects of war
against those of innocence
who should be friends
far from hated enemies
but for a nations flag
of dedicated allegiance

~ Ed Woods

What I Remember

Shaky hands
that could
never learn to drive.

Sleepless nights,
thirty years on,
from shrapnel particles in his side.

Marching in the rain
at the vets parade in 1985.

Cold beer and Glenn Miller
at the Legion on Friday nights.

The indescribable moment
when his son graduated from
The Royal Military College.

His smiling face.

The poppies encircling his coffin,
and the men who played him out,
on pipes of glory.

~ John Sweeney

Port Chicago

Railroad cars above satin white ballast,
hidden in casket shaped hillocks,
buried fragments, guarding secrets,
whispered across generations. A pall
of wildflowers purple the bulwark sides,
concealing memories of mass destruction.

The magazine dressed in ice plant greens,
pinned with rusty quills, leaving
 rusty bleeds of forgotten jobs:
containing blasts and discharging electricity.
A boxcar rests in peace, between revetment walls.
It is the silence of the tomb.

Death has stolen our voice.
Our DNA vaporized on a summer night.
The fossors stand empty-handed.
The air is moist with forgetfulness.
The miasma of dead bodies lingers in the evaporation.

Our bodies born up; effluvium to cloud ledges,
coating airplane windows: Amelios potamos.
The water birds scuttle the top of Suisan Bay,

crying for the children, living only in the memory
of names etched in granite. S2c Eddie L Cross,
S2c Jessie V Crump, M3c Clarence S Fields...

War has no children, just thoughts that live
in the brains of mighty young men,
Expendable and sacrificed in careless disregard.

An accident of afterbirth and after death.

"I am injured in my spine but that is nothing compared with my
many friends who have been blown into forgetfulness."
Joseph Crosby

        ~ Barbara A. Meier

          Previously published in 2017 "Here Comes Everyone"

North America's New War

The hostile breath of war
inhales and exhales
in black and white under metal gray

Frontiersmen knowingly wait
for gunfire, bombs, the lethal germ,
singing freedom songs gallantly forged from dust.

No uniforms expose the enemy.
No heavy boots parade shaky, neutral grounds.

Angry faces shout anti-American slurs,
worship posters of Hitler in a beard,
sport suicide vests under accouterments of hate,
call themselves oppressed heroes.

Cube vans with tinted windows
race on deconstructed roads at 2 a.m.,
transport harbingers of death to hidden laboratories.

The militia murders joggers, airline passengers,
children in school yards and universities,
coffee house patrons, subway & bus travelers,
and afterwards,

throw parties and celebrate their victories
and pay homage to a sinister god.

~ I. B. Iskov

A Decima for the Doughboys

Influenced by the zealous praise
coming from teachers and parents
they left enthused before real sense
replaced the glow of youthful gaze,
pride, and honor with true malaise.
Troops become a sacrifice for
Mars, depleting their thirst for war.
Instead of music and parades,
a drumbeat of cannon cascades
into the trenches of world war.

~ Bill Cushing

Standing In The Shadows
for my Dad

growing up in the shadow of a giant
granite strong impervious to all
I waded into adulthood swaddled with young
entrenched with long nights and close calls

men and women stand
in the rain always in the rain
wrapped tightly in their gloom
awash in foreign lands --
a red poppy given out by these old veterans
unknown warriors
strangers in front of Wal-Mart
as they stand in the shadows
with droplets falling

reaching the entrance
I see my father's eyes
in every old man's face

I remember the few stories he shared
about the pain and fear
the long nights lost fights
close calls and sacrifice by - hoping he'd done enough
hoping his grandchildren won't ever have to

~ Trish Shields

The Gallery's Black Watch

A watercolour hangs for exhibition,
a crucifixion, mass murder
    >in/of<   dreams,
while on the shooting gallery floor
the tragedy of maple leaves
pleading for salvation
    and Verriere's Second Coming:

those human sacrifices,
their fading impressions
like felled wheat blades enshrined
in a harvest of blood-choked brush—
    the Black Watch.

In this gallery, fossilized by time,
a nightmare and its prayers survive
beside a thieves' hill top
and a miscalculated messiah
surveys the poppied mass

    ... Lest we forget.

    ~ Ronda Wicks Eller

The Battle of Verrières Ridge was a series of engagements fought as part of the Battle of Normandy, in Calvados, during WWII. The main combatants were two Canadian infantry divisions against elements of three German SS Panzer divisions. The high ground was held by the Germans but Canadian and British forces made repeated attempts to capture the ridge for six days. This battle is remembered for a highly controversial order to attack during which The Black Watch (Royal Highland Regiment) of Canada had 315 of its 325 soldiers killed, wounded or captured.

Lancaster Bombers

four big engines
thunder the sky
to defend freedom

a beautiful machine
built by talented workers
who seldom ever see
post-production damage

~ Ed Woods

Covert Sniper

across the way
my enemy kill-shot

children play in the foreground

one bullet
must make it through
to the Commander
a dream challenge target

there is no rush
they are camped out

no matter
the collateral damage
he must fall dead
laser sighted dead

~Ed Woods

Lucky Man

Days to go -- two-o-eight--
until the sweet bird swoops and
plucks me from this
benighted place before
dark messengers intervene

Rick the Tease
I am the short-timer!*
I am FIGMO!**
I am 18 days and a wakeup
I am Lucky Man...
until an eerie whine
awakens ghosts, then
impulsively explodes,
sending rampaging shards
of red-hot shrapnel
tumbling headlong

Cascaded into terror,
ears concussed, eyes dust-filled,
spurting blood stipples my face,
splatters across my chest,
a cocktail from the dark messenger?
one for whose road? whose last call?

Lucky Man...until his lank body
shredded, sickeningly splayed about,
scooped into a black rubber cocoon
Once the Lucky Man...now he goes
to his rest too soon

Grief and guilt whirl
in my mind's maelstrom,
unable to decipher
the impenetrable mystery
how bombs and rockets
and shells and bullets
name their victims

Another Lucky Man tomorrow,
but not my tomorrow
for two-o-seven remain

before Lucky Man's mantle
drapes my shoulders

~ Mark Fleisher

* short-timer: having a few days left in his/her tour of duty in
Vietnam
* FIGMO: acronym for F**k, I Got My Orders (orders for going
home)

*Previously published in Moments of Time (2014), Mercury
Heartlink, Albuquerque and Silver City, NM, USA*

Drowning in Retreat in 1991

With the battle lost, those few who
survived buried themselves

under sand, dug in only to get
bulldozed beneath a front stretching

across 170 miles
of parched shoreline. Did these Iraqi

sons and fathers, pawns praying
to Allah, beg or shout for mercy

over the thrum of diesel engines
like surf drumming in the desert.

What god could've heard the screams
of these conscripts coming from

under those granular waves?
All noise is muffled as throats and lungs

filled with that smothering tide.
Their blood, seeping into the grains,

makes its own mud, and they—
the men never really wanting

to be there—fall victim to this,
a new and unintended assault.

~ Bill Cushing

On Navy Seas

The one lonely gull above the navy sea,
flickers of light from the offing, the curvature
of the earth a degree below the horizon, smoky haze
from the stack and the wake - a path to twilight.

The silence lies about peace and brings to mind
the loneliness of one amongst the ghosts.

Death lives forever in damaged cells,
missile silos, and burning C130's.
War makes mutes of men, the gas of tears
searing the lining of their throats.
The fellowship of the dead,
the silence of the navy sea
and one lone gull.
Cum tacent, clamant!

When they are silent they shout!
Cicero

~ Barbara A. Meier

First published in 2017," Poppy Road Review"

The Cemetery Has Its Stories

At the edge of the cemetery
the spring creeks swell and spill over.
They crisscross the uneven ground
and cause havoc with boundaries.
They soak the earth and topple the monuments
before they return to their babbling.

The graves of the veterans are silent.
They took their stories with them.
Their families never speak
of the cries in the night
or the grey mornings
when even birdsong was too loud.

We have to dredge the ditches
if we want to know the truth
of what really happened
on those battlefields.
The cemetery has its stories.
but they are written in mud
hidden by poppies
and it takes generations before they swell
into words, and spill over
into poems.

~ Wendy MacLean

Under The Leaden Sky

The cold crudely clumps inside wind
on brutal nights,
ices labyrinths in the dark.

Six-pointed stars arrested,
sealed in principled prisons,
await liberation
- stoic underground movements.

Fragile, precious
antique silver mezuzahs
behind barbed wire fences;
careful reactions pattern shame.

The authority of order
mighty as a skyscraper,
stubborn as a hurricane,
stalwart as a terrorist.

I fight City Hall,
demand mountains be climbed,
insist concrete airplanes
be awarded less gravity.

I want to wade through the windy warren
while naked parchment whimpers
timeless through dark dreams
in a secret spring.

~ I. B. Iskov

The Last Farewell

Wearily breathe she slept
Safe as the secrets she kept
"Don't leave me behind" I whispered
Frames of memories lingered

With a blank stare I wondered
If she would greet her mother
Dews on my lashes I prayed
We would live to see the parade

Hunting shadows parted the stygian sky
Echoed the sooted copper bell rang
Wooden suitcase was my disgrace
And for the last time, we embraced

~ Amberyx

Going Home

when will I go home
the more I ask
the more I am brushed off
this place is no longer joyful

day after day
wheelchair travel fades
in comparison to my fighter plane
propeller whirling exhaust cackle
test fire wing canons
my armored seat shakes
cushioned by a parachute
adrenaline ready to defend freedom
upon green light clearance

now I wear a faceless watch
around my ankle and wrist
a nuisance gift of generosity
that I will not disrespect
as staff truly care for many in need

this afternoon the receptionist
promised an answer
as to when I will go home

~ Ed Woods

A Sonnet to Slaughter

The ground held no value, the town little use,
except for foot-rotted, grey-clad men
hoping to find much-needed shoes.
What followed was beyond their ken
when groves of peach trees and fields of wheat
became hallowed witness to brutalities
as lice-ridden troops, bound for defeat,
charged over meadows and fallen bodies.
The banshee wail of the rebel yell
arose with bayonets and shot lead;
cannonade shook buildings, roof tiles fell,
and after three days, desperation led
Gettysburg, then a place of little worth—
now one of lost causes, "a perfect hell on earth."

~ Bill Cushing

Inspired by the diary of Robert H. Carter, private: 22nd
Massachusetts infantry

Milestones

young men
left their farms
in war effort pride
to show an enemy
rural justice
a quick war
no losses
then home
to celebration

but all nationalities fell
onto the ground
inside equipment
and from the sky

deep embedded horror
lasted long after armistice
heavy tears fall
in many a beer mug
cocktail glass
and saturate pillows
old era photos
stop daily activities
X'd out military members
some from natural causes

post war success
health and possessions
country drives to picnic
the best of technology
in every home

today the war-aged
enjoy youthful liberties

fruition of my effort
roosted a milestone
as in today's mail
arrived the first
veteran's cheque

~ Ed Woods

Understanding Toward "The Other"

hatred toward "the other" is nurtured in fear
roiling and boiling within inner forces
curdling empathy in creative sources
rarely reading nor flying away
to immerse in new cultures and worlds
but only go places where one's flag is unfurled
evolution's made up; the ark is what sails
global warming is senseless; it's only a fraud
climate change is decided by one's own Christian god

research and facts are rarely respected
the rapture will save us which one awaits
scientists know little; instead there's pure faith
so we know, in our self-defined state
facts are distortions to be shot down in flames
our truths are determined by unshakeable claims
minds are made up; no one else can decide
reality's complete with salvation our guide
in this cocoon of a world resistant to change.

~ Lisa Makarchuk

To understand the mindset of what leads to racism and an
ideology of race supremacy

The Sweater

Home from the war, Dad moved back
with his folks in their old stone house
on Queen Street East, Hespeler.

One night, he sat having tea with Grandma,
while she sorted out the laundry,
all set for morning chores.

She pulled a tawny wool sweater
with a thick rolled collar from the pile,
asked, "Where did you get this?"

In Aldershot, he replied, from a Red Cross Depot.
I needed something warm to wear under my tunic.

He explained how he'd given his greatcoat
to his big Bren gunner, before leaving the front
to be decorated by King George VI,
at Buckingham Palace.

Big greatcoats
were in sharp demand by the war's end.
He added, It was cold and damp in Aldershot
that spring of '45. So I picked this sweater.

"I knitted this sweater," said Grandma.
Dad chuckled, No, Ma, there were hundred
of sweaters there, piles of them. I just liked this one.

Grandma picked up her sewing scissors, snipped back
the sweater's rolled collar, and pulled out a two dollar bill,
and a 'Dear Soldier' letter written in her hand.

During the war, Grandma, like countless
other Canadian women, had regularly knitted
scarves, mitts, hats and sweaters, and donated them
to the Red Cross to be sent to soldiers overseas.

Throughout her life, Grandma had kept up
correspondence with many returned soldiers
who had felt something stiff and crumply
inside those collars.

There were hundred of sweaters there, Mom.
Hundreds...

~ Becky Alexander

Previously published in "Shrapnel, Tales of a Soldier Dad" by Becky Alexander, Craigleigh Press, Cambridge ON, 2009.

About the Poets

Alexander, Becky
Becky Alexander has been writing poetry for three decades. As a member of five poetry societies she has won over 300 contest awards in Canada and the United States and is the publisher of the micro publishing company Craigleigh Press.

Allard, Donna
Donna is International Beat Poet Laureate (2019-20) for the National Beat Poetry Foundation Inc., CT, U.S.A., the founding editor of River Bones Press and now curates Canadian Beat Scene. She's a peaceful "purdyesque" writer from New Brunswick, Canada.

Amberyx
Amberyx has always had a passion for creative writing. She is an outdoor enthusiast and loves to find inspiration in nature. In addition to writing she also enjoys ballet, classical music and visual arts. She is currently an undergraduate science student at the University of Western Ontario.

Cushing, Bill
Called the "blue collar poet" by peers at the University of Central Florida, Bill Cushing is related to Lt. Alonzo Cushing, an artillery commander killed while repelling Pickett's Charge at the Battle of Gettysburg. Earning an MFA from Goddard College, his book, A Former Life, is available from Finishing Line Press.

Delaney, David J.
Leaving school at 15, three months into grade 8, has challenged David's literary ventures, which began in late December 2007 (being primarily self-taught posed a huge learning curve) but in poetry and memoire/short story writing, he's had wonderful support (Australian and worldwide). He says, "If I inspire one person to write or showcase their work, I've done my job".

Fleisher, Mark
Mark Fleisher is an Albuquerque, New Mexico-based writer who has published three books of poetry and collaborated on a fourth. He holds a journalism degree from Ohio University. His United States Air Force service included a year in Vietnam as a combat news reporter.

Freer, Meg

Meg Freer grew up in Montana and lives in Kingston, Ontario. She has worked as an editor and currently teaches piano and music history. She enjoys running and being outdoors year-round and wishes she had more time for writing poetry. Her writing has been published in various journals and anthologies.

Iskov, I. B. (Bunny)

Bunny is the Founder of The Ontario Poetry Society. Her work has been published in many fine literary journals and anthologies. She has three full collections and several chapbooks. She is available for readings and workshops upon request. Bunny is married to Larry and they have two children, one son-in-law and two grandchildren.

MacKenzie, Bob

Bob was born and raised in western Canada; he lives in Kingston, Ontario. Influenced by the cold war and the ever-present invasions and skirmishes common around the world from then until now, he has written often about war's personal and cultural effects. His war poems are triggered by the tragedy it inflicts on soldiers but also on everyone it touches.

MacLean, Wendy

Wendy Jean MacLean is an award-winning poet with a huge capacity for wonder. Her work has been published in Canada, UK, USA and Japan. More than thirty of her poems have been set to music and sung across the country. She is a minister in a small country church in Eastern Ontario.

Makarchuk, Lisa

Lisa co-coordinated the First and Third International Festivals of Poetry of Resistance. She has published a chapter in a collection of essays in Cuba Solidarity in Canada. Her issue-oriented poetry is found in anthologies; her poetry is in "Bottom of the Wine Jar" published by the CCLA.

Meier, Barbara A.

Barbara A Meier has spent the last four years living on the Southern Oregon Coast. She retired from teaching this summer and hopes to find time to travel and write. Her first Micro Chapbook, "Wildfire LAL 6" came out this summer from Ghost City Press. She has been published in "The Poeming Pigeon", TD; LR "Catching Fire Anthology" and "The Fourth River". https://basicallybarbmeier.wordpress.com/

Shields, Trish

Trish Shields has had two books of poetry published and her poetry and short stories have been featured in international anthologies. Trish spends her time as an editor and freelance photographer. She is currently working on a manuscript about genocide - the faces change but the remains stay the same.

Stones, David

David Stones is a poet and spoken word performer residing in both Toronto and Stratford, Ontario. He performs his one-man poetry-based show, Infinite Sequels, throughout southern Ontario. David's poetry has been published widely, with over 30 poems published in the past year in magazines and journals from Canada to France to India.

Sweeney, John

John is a surviving drama teacher and theatre director who enjoys writing poetry. His favourite play about war is Journey's End (Sherriff), novel: The Wars (Findley), and poem: Drummer Hodge(Hardy). His father was a proud Canadian veteran of The Second World War and a great dad.

Warner, Barrett

Barrett Warner is the author of "Why Is It So Hard to Kill You?" (Somondoco, 2016) and "My Friend Ken Harvey" (Publishing Genius, 2014). He lives along the upper reach of the South Edisto River in South Carolina.

Whitfield, Vanessa Rowan

Vanessa Rowan Whitfield is an American artist. Her work has been shared for the last decade in galleries, on local television, international podcasts, in international magazines and anthologies. She lost her cousin Brendan, who lived with her as a brother in 2014, to suicide after he served in Iraq.

Wicks Eller, Ronda

Ronda has two chapbooks, four trade books and four novels in publication. Her work has been featured in anthologies and journals internationally, and she's the owner (and "Jane of all trades") for SkyWing Press based in Huron-Perth, Ontario, Canada. Ronda is a Branch Manager for T.O.P.S. and an Editor for Canadian Beat Scene.

Youden, Philip

Philip Youden is a graduate of Mount Allison University where he received a Bachelor of Science in Biology. He lives in Petitcodiac, New Brunswick and writes part time.

www.ingramcontent.com/pod-product-compliance
Lightning Source LLC
Chambersburg PA
CBHW032029040426
42448CB00006B/773